Airplanes

By Hal Rogers

The Child's World®, Inc.

Published by The Child's World®, Inc.
PO Box 326
Chanhassen, MN 55317-0326
800-599-READ
www.childsworld.com

Design and Production:
The Creative Spark, San Juan Capistrano, CA

Photos: © 2000 David M. Budd Photography

We thank Frontier Airlines for their help in preparing this book.

Library of Congress Cataloging-in-Publication Data

Rogers, Hal, 1966-
    Airplanes / by Hal Rogers.
       p. cm.
    ISBN 1-56766-962-X
     1. Airplanes—Juvenile literature. [1. Airplanes.] I. Title.
    TL547 .R58 2000
    629.133'340423—dc21

                           00-011372

Contents

On the Job

On the job, airplanes carry people and things from place to place. They fly high up in the sky.

Passengers go to the airport.

A worker takes their tickets when

it's time to **board.**

The passengers walk down the **jetway.** It is a long, narrow hallway. It takes them to the airplane.

The **cabin** is where the passengers

sit. They enter through a big door.

There are many seats in the cabin.
Passengers can put small bags in
the **bins** above their seats.

Workers load bigger things into the **baggage compartment.** It is below the cabin.

Sometimes passengers take their
pets with them. Dogs and cats travel
in special boxes. They travel below
the cabin, too.

The airplane has wings made of sturdy metal. It also has powerful engines. This airplane has two engines, one on each side.

The airplane also has a tail. The wings and the tail have **flaps.** The tail flap moves from side to side.

The wing flaps move up and down.

The flaps work with the engines to

make the airplane fly.

Fasten your seat belts! We're headed for the **runway.** The runway is a long strip of road. Airplanes use runways when they take off and land.

Now it's time for takeoff.

Climb Aboard!

Would you like to see where the **pilot** sits? The pilot sits in the **cockpit.** He uses **controls** to fly the airplane. Some controls move the wing and tail flaps. Others make the plane go faster or slower. Controls also make the plane go higher and lower. The pilot uses the **yoke** to steer the airplane.

19

Up Close

The inside

The cockpit

1. The controls

2. The yoke

3. The pilot's seat

The cabin

4. The bins

5. The passenger seats

The outside

1. The jetway

2. The tail

3. The cockpit

4. The door

5. The wings

6. The engine

7. The baggage compartment

Glossary

baggage compartment (BAG-edj kum-PART-ment)
A baggage compartment is a place to store suitcases and other large items. Airplanes have a baggage compartment below the cabin.

bins (BINZ)
Bins are places where people store things. An airplane has bins inside the cabin.

board (BORD)
When people board an airplane, they get on it. People use a jetway to board an airplane.

cabin (KAB-in)
A cabin is the space inside an airplane where passengers sit. An airplane cabin has many seats.

cockpit (KOK-pit)
A cockpit is the place in an airplane where the pilot sits. An airplane's controls are in the cockpit.

controls (kun-TROLZ)
Controls are buttons, switches, and other tools that make a machine work. A pilot uses controls to fly an airplane.

flaps (FLAPZ)
On an airplane, flaps are moveable parts on the wings and tail. Airplane flaps move up and down or from side to side.

jetway (JET-way)
A jetway is a long hallway between an airport and an airplane. Passengers board the airplane through the jetway.

passengers (PASS-en-jerz)
Passengers are travelers in vehicles such as airplanes, cars, or buses. Passengers ride in the cabin of an airplane.

pilot (PY-lut)
The person who drives an airplane is called the pilot. The pilot works the airplane's controls.

runway (RUN-way)
A runway is a strip of land on which airplanes take off and land. An airplane travels down a runway before takeoff.

yoke (YOHK)
A yoke is a control used to steer an airplane. A yoke is like the steering wheel of a car.